A QUESTION A DAY

KEEPS

THE BOREDOM AWAY

By

Nayden Kostov

Contents

PROLOGUE

This book provides you with fun and challenging questions, whether you want to quiz yourself or your family. Learn something new every day and surprise your circle of friends and colleagues!

Knowing stuff makes you a cool and interesting interlocutor. You will always have an icebreaker at hand to start a conversation or to keep it going by dropping a weird fact.

I covered a wide range of topics and intentionally made the questions assorted, so you will not know what sort of fact is coming. As I would do myself, you can choose to read as many facts as you please in one sitting, or even just one fact each day!

You could use this collection when preparing for a pub quiz or quiz night at work or at home. All the questions are well-researched and family-friendly. Become a trivia whiz with even more facts in the Hard to Believe Facts series!

JANUARY

1 January

A chemical compound called "castoreum" is used in flavoured foods. As its name suggests, it is extracted from beavers. More precisely, from beavers' anal glands. Which natural flavour does it substitute?

Vanilla

2 January

In Japan, surnames became obligatory in which year?

1875

3 January

When it was founded, Harvard did not teach calculus (the branch of mathematics). Why?

It was not yet invented

4 January

Except for humans, how many animals have a chin?

0. Even the Neanderthals did not have a chin

5 January

Monster trucks first appeared in which year?

1981

6 January

In 2021, Kataluna Enriquez was crowned Miss Nevada (USA). Why did she attract media interest from all over the world?

She was the first transgender woman to win

7 January

How many people have been hit by a meteorite so far?

1 (in 1954, in the USA)

8 January

Romania has virtually the same flag as which country?

Chad

9 January

What do the names of the countries Bolivia, Colombia, Liechtenstein, The Philippines, Saudi Arabia, Mauritius, Seychelles, and Cambodia have in common?

They were all named after people

10 January

Where is shamanism a popular religion?

Mongolia

11 January

Through how many countries does the Equator pass?

13

12 January

What is the dot over the letter "i" called?

A tittle

13 January

What is the Fahrenheit equivalent of 0°C?

32°F

14 January

On the island of La Gomera (one of the Canary Islands, Spain) the traditional local language is taught at school. What is the peculiarity of this language?

The Silbo Gomero is a whistling language

15 January

All mammals, with the exception of two species, have seven neck vertebrae. Could you name any of the exceptions?

Sloths and manatees

16 January

In the past, most doctors worldwide thought that babies could not feel pain. Therefore, many surgeries were performed on infants without anaesthesia. When did it change?

1986

17 January

What is the exact Latin equivalent of the word "interesting"?

There is none

18 January

How many days make up a non-leap year in the Islamic calendar?

354

19 January

Sergei Krikalev was a Soviet astronaut who was in space when the USSR was dissolved. Upon his return to Earth a few months later, the media called him "the last Soviet citizen". How many days has he spent in space in his entire career? Hint: he is #3 in the world...

803 days

20 January

Avocado was considered by the Aztecs to be an aphrodisiac. The word "avocado" comes from the Aztec word "ahuácatl", which means what? Hint: part of humans' reproductive system.

Testicle

21 January

The Shinkansen, also known as the bullet train, is a network of high-speed railway lines in Japan. It started in 1964 and has transported over 10 billion passengers. What is the total number of passengers who have died in train accidents involving Shinkansen so far?

0

22 January

Initially, bowling pins had to be re-set between rounds by humans, hired as "professional alley pinsetters". When was the process automated?

1936

23 January

Wikipedia derives from "wiki" from the Hawaiian "wikiwiki" + "pedia" from "encyclopedia". What does wiki mean in Hawaiian?

Rapid

24 January

The only ancient culture to develop a word for "blue" was?

Ancient Egypt

25 January

Which sport (performed by men only) requires that the sportsmen be at least 167 cm (5.5 ft.) tall, and weigh a minimum of 67 kg (148 lb)?

Sumo (according to Japan Times, 2019)

26 January

The releasing of doves at the Olympics began in 1920 as a symbolic gesture of peace following the end of WWI. Doves were used at the opening of each game until an unfortunate incident put an end to it. At one opening ceremony, some of the doves were attracted to the Olympic torch and ended up being burnt alive. When and where did it happen?

1988, Seoul

27 January

The Pacific Ocean is how many times wider than the Moon?

5 times

28 January

In most situations where we would put our initials or signatures on a document, the Japanese do something else. It is called *hanko* or *inkan*. Explain what it is.

It is a personal stamp

29 January

Which were the last Olympic Games to have an official cigarette sponsor?

Los Angeles, 1984

30 January

Some time ago, India and Sri Lanka used to be connected by a strip of land called Adam's Bridge (aka Rama's Bridge or Rama Setu). People could walk over this land bridge on foot until a cyclone destroyed the bridge, turning it into a chain of reefs. When did this cyclone happen?

In 1480 CE

31 January

Thomas salto and Korbut flip/Mukhina flip are gymnastics skills that are presently banned. Why were they banned?

They were deemed too dangerous

FEBRUARY

1 February

What percentage of the coral reefs worldwide are expected to survive if the water in oceans warms by 3°C?

0%

2 February

Ketchup is usually based on tomato paste. In the Philippines, however, there is a very popular sort of ketchup based on a different plant. What fruit or vegetable do they use?

Bananas

3 February

In one African country, the controversial tradition of "leblouh" (force-feeding girls before marriage) is still alive. Preteen girls are forced to ingest up to 15,000 calories each day (four times the daily ration of a male bodybuilder) because of the widespread belief that obese brides are more desirable. Name the country.

Mauritania

4 February

During the Cold War, hundreds of American spies were caught in the USSR because their fake passports were easy to spot. What were the fake passports missing that real ones had?

The US fakes used stainless steel staples, while the ones used in real passports got rusty really quickly

5 February

How do manatees control their buoyancy?

They pass gas

6 February

When you are bitten by a venomous snake, you need the antidote. Snake venom antidotes are produced by injecting small portions of venom inside which animal?

Horses

7 February

In 1972, tennis balls were made yellow/green so that they would be better visible on TV. What colour were they before 1972?

White or black

8 February

Name the largest country with one time zone.

China

9 February

Espresso coffee was patented in Turin, Italy. In which year?

1884

10 February

How many times has the United Kingdom's Queen Elizabeth II addressed the general public so far, except for the annual end-of-year speech?

Only 5

11 February

Which was the first country to adopt Bitcoin as a legal tender?

El Salvador

12 February

In an effort to improve the linguistic lives of all English speakers, the Czech Republic registered its short-form name, Czechia. What year did it happen?

In 2016, the name was officially registered with the United Nations

13 February

On 27 July 1953, Communist and United Nations delegates signed an armistice ending the Korean War. How many words did the delegates exchange in total during this event?

Nobody spoke a word and there were no handshakes

14 February

The Soviet prototype V-12 (Mi-12) is the largest helicopter ever built. It still holds the record of lifting 40 tons to an altitude of 2,255m (7,400 ft.) It was capable of transporting how many passengers?

196

15 February

What distinctive colour are the taxis in Mexico City?

Pink

16 February

On 16 February 1568, the Spanish Inquisition issued a death sentence to all residents of which country?

The Netherlands

17 February

The mole (*Talpa europaea*) can be found throughout Europe but not in which European mainland country?

Norway. It is not present either in island countries such as Northern Ireland and Republic of Ireland, Malta, and Cyprus

18 February

Why do coins have ridges?

There are two major reasons: ridges make coins harder to fake and prevent shaving – i.e. cutting tiny parts off the coin

19 February

Which is the only German-speaking country that shares no border with Germany?

Liechtenstein

20 February

The shape of these beer bottles is a bit unusual (see photo). They are specially designed in a way that after drinking the beer, one could use the empty bottle for what?

They can be used as bricks

21 February

Liechtenstein used to have the same flag as Haiti. It was only discovered during the Olympic Games in what year or country?

1936, Berlin. Then Liechtenstein decided to add a coat of arms to the flag

22 February

US astronaut, John Young, is famous for his Apollo 16 moonwalks and his role as commander of the first space shuttle mission. His mission, Gemini 3, however, was accompanied by a scandal as he smuggled something unauthorized in space. What did he secretly bring aboard?

A sandwich

23 February

Several countries geographically outside Europe have competed in the Eurovision Song Contest so far: Israel, Morocco, and most recently, which country?

Australia

24 February

Bitche is a town in France's Grand Est region. Recently, its Facebook page was automatically deleted by bots. Why?

Wrongly captured as the English "bitch" and hence perceived as offensive

25 February

Which European capital used to be named Kristiania until 1925?

Oslo

26 February

The F-35 aircraft is the most expensive weapon in history, with a projected lifetime cost of $1.7 trillion. That's more than Russia's GDP, all spent on a single-seat plane. If this US aircraft were a country, its GDP would rank at which place in the world?

11th (presently occupied by Russia)

27 February

In May 2021, the World Health Organization warned against using one particular cow product, which many Indians rub onto their bodies in hope of protection against COVID-19. Which product?

Manure

28 February

In New York City, tattoo studios were illegal until which year?

1997

29 February

What is the most common colour for country flags?

Red

MARCH

1 March

The Colossus of Rhodes was a colossal statue of a Greek god that stood in the ancient Greek city of Rhodes and was one of the Seven Wonders of the World. Which god was depicted?

Helios, the God of Sun

2 March

US businessman, Dennis Tito, became history's first space tourist, paying his own way to the International Space Station aboard a Russian Soyuz spacecraft. In which year?

2001

3 March

When Coca-Cola started production in Bulgaria, for the first time, its logo was presented in the Cyrillic alphabet. In which year did it happen?

1965

4 March

For his day job at the newspaper, The Daily Planet, Superman is paid by another superhero. Who technically pays Superman's salary?

Batman (Bruce Wayne)

5 March

Which is the only European country to have had a capital city outside Europe in the 19th century?

Portugal, Rio de Janeiro. Turkey's capital, Ankara, is indeed in Asia, but only since 1923

6 March

What does the abbreviation CNN stand for?

Cable News Network

7 March

In 1885, the Congo Free State, an area larger than Belgium, was established under King Leopold II's personal rule and private army, the Force Publique. How many times larger than Belgium was this colony?

76 times

8 March

In early 2021, which country became the only country in the world with both a female President and a female Prime Minister?

Estonia

9 March

The national anthem of which country is, in fact, two different songs put together with five of the official languages being used?

South Africa

10 March

Which country is the most mentioned in the national anthems of other countries?

Spain holds this record with 13 mentions. France is in second place with 8

11 March

Over the centuries, the rulers of one country have founded dozens of new capitals to mark a new dynasty or a new reign, to shift to a safer or more fertile ground, or simply to follow the advice of astrologers. The last capital change (ostensibly on an astrologer's advice) happened in 2005/2006. Name the country.

Myanmar

12 March

Which famous professional boxer was nominated for the Grammy awards twice?

Muhammad Ali

13 March

Who is the largest tyre producer in the world?

Lego

14 March

How many distinct giraffe species are living today?

Up until recently, the consensus has been there is only one species of giraffe with multiple subspecies. In 2016, a study found genetic differences among giraffe populations, indicating the existence of four distinct giraffe species

15 March

When was the first dot com domain in the world, Symbolics.com, registered?

On 15 March 1985

16 March

According to 2020 data, US music lovers are spending more money on vinyl records than CDs. This has happened for the first time since which year?

1986

17 March

Nigel Richards (born 1967) is among the most successful Scrabble players of all time. In 2015, Richards won the French World Scrabble Championship. At the time, media all over the world reported this fact as something exceptional and sensational as he was sort of "disadvantaged" compared to other participants. What was his "disadvantage"?

He did not speak French, but successfully memorized all French words

18 March

The highest jump with a parachute was made by Felix Baumgartner in 2012. From what altitude did he jump?

21,818 metres (71,581 ft.)

19 March

The deepest swimming pool is in Dubai, UAE. What is its depth?

60m (197 ft.)

20 March

The etymology of the word bankruptcy is a bit weird as it comes from the Italian "banca rotta", that is "broken desk" (or similar), owing to the habit in the Middle Ages of breaking the desk of the insolvent banker. In which Italian city did it originate?

Florence

21 March

In 2019, US President Donald Trump offered Denmark to buy which big island?

Greenland

22 March

"Go away! Last words are for fools who haven't said enough!" are the last words of who?

Karl Marx

23 March

The largest swimming pool is in which country?

Egypt: Citystars Sharm El Sheikh,
96,800 m2 (1,042,000 sq. ft.)

24 March

The Catalburun, Pachon Navarro, and Andean Tiger Hound are the only three dog breeds that possess a strange body feature: they have one body part split in two. Which one?

They have a split nose

25 March

Coca-Cola's recipe is kept in a bank safe. Where? (Name the city or the US state.)

Atlanta, Georgia

26 March

Which country has the longest-serving central bank
governor (for over 30 years now)?

*Romania, Constantin Mugur Isărescu (born 1 August
1949) is the Governor of the National Bank of
Romania, a position he held since September 1990,
with the exception of an eleven-month period (16
November 1999 to 28 October 2000), during which he
served as Prime Minister of Romania*

27 March

Which is the first country in the world to offer a
frequent visitors rewards program?

*Maldives introduced their frequent visitors program
in September 2020*

28 March

A large statue of Felipe III in Madrid, Spain, is responsible for the death of hundreds of birds. Why?

When the statue was first made, the horse's mouth was open. Birds used to fly into it and would not be able to get out, so they would die inside. They replaced the statue with a horse with a closed mouth

29 March

Braille is a tactile writing system for people who are visually impaired. It codes each letter of the alphabet using how many dots?

6 dots. Additional fact: Braille was based on a tactile military code called "night writing", developed by Charles Barbier in response to Napoleon's demand for a means for soldiers to communicate silently at night and without a light source. In Barbier's system, sets of 12 embossed dots encoded 36 different sounds. It proved to be too difficult for soldiers to recognize by touch and was rejected by the military

30 March

Redheads (people with red hair) need more anaesthesia to be sedated. Do you know how much more (by percent)?

About 20%

31 March

Everyone has heard of the Seven Wonders of the Ancient World listed by the Hellenic culture. However, we do not know the exact location of one of them. Moreover, we are not entirely sure if it even existed. Which one?

The Hanging Gardens of Babylon

APRIL

1 April

The FBI's Ten Most Wanted Fugitives is a most wanted list maintained by the United States FBI. When was it first published?

1950

2 April

What percentage of Earth's mass is water?

Water mass is 0.02% of our planet

3 April

How many people have walked on the Moon?

12

4 April

Stone money, known as Rai, are large doughnut-shaped and carved stone disks that measure up to 4m (13 ft.) in diameter and weigh up to 4 tonnes. Name a country where they were or still are in use.

Micronesia, Palau, Guam (USA)

5 April

Douglas Engelbart invented the computer mouse. When did he build the first working prototype?

1964

6 April

Do you know why that extra scrap of cloth is included in new clothes?

They are given so that you do not wash it in a way that can potentially ruin your entire dress. You can check it by washing the sample using a washing powder or bleach to know if it will shrink or change colour

7 April

Which is the largest fish with a bone skeleton?

Moonfish

8 April

The Church of the Flying Spaghetti Monster is also known as what?

Pastafarianism

9 April

In April 2019, Serbia advised its citizens to avoid travelling to one European country due to "major political chaos". Which country?

The United Kingdom

10 April

Queen Victoria was the British monarch from 1837 to 1901. She had a living grandchild until which year?

1981

11 April

Which was the last nation to put a flag on the Moon?

China

12 April

In one European country, all new PhD graduates are given a sword and a hat during the official ceremony. Name the country.

Finland

13 April

Tom Cruise has divorced all his wives when they turned what age?

33

14 April

The American Service-Members' Protection Act authorizes the US President to use military force for the release of any US or allied personnel being detained or imprisoned by, on behalf of, or at the request of the International Criminal Court. This authorization was nicknamed the "Hague Invasion Act". When was it passed?

2002

15 April

Which gemstone has the simplest chemical composition?

Diamond

16 April

How many boxes does a typical Sudoku puzzle have?

81

17 April

You only have two body parts that never stop growing.
Name them.

Nose and ears

18 April

In one Asian country, the President banned black cars
from the capital city because he believes white brings
good luck. Which country?

Turkmenistan

19 April

In October 2020, Lucio Chiquito from Medellín,
Colombia, submitted his PhD thesis at the age of 104. He
had started his PhD long ago. Do you know how many
years ago?

77 years ago

20 April

On most airplane safety cards, there is only one word on the pictures. Which word?

"Exit"

21 April

What is Donald Trump's middle name?

John

22 April

An Austrian village called Fucking has just changed its name to what?

Fugging

23 April

In which country is the present capital's name an anagram of the previous capital's name?

Japan (Tokyo-Kyoto)

24 April

Mc is an abbreviation of Gaelic Mac, meaning what?

"Son"

25 April

Most passenger airplanes are painted white for a practical reason. Why?

The white paint is lighter

26 April

The siege of Weinsberg happened in 1140 CE, in the modern state of Baden-Württemberg, Germany. The attacking king made a deal for the surrender of the castle stating that the women were free to leave, taking with them anything they would be able to carry on their backs. What did women take on their backs?

Their husbands

27 April

Liechtenstein gave women suffrage last in Europe. In which year?

In 1984

28 April

Modern Sudoku was invented in 1979, but the game did not take off until it was introduced in Japan in what year?

In 1984

29 April

Liechtenstein last went to war in 1866, sending 80 soldiers to Italy. How many soldiers returned?

81. It is unclear if the extra man was an Austrian liaison officer or an Italian defector

30 April

When was "Ciabatta" bread invented?

1982

MAY

1 May

What does each letter in RAP (as in rap music) stand for?

Rhythm and poetry

2 May

What does each letter in TED stand for?

Technology, Entertainment, Design

3 May

Which is the biggest fish in the ocean?

The Rhincodon typus or whale shark

4 May

Which country is the world's heaviest consumer of beer?

Czech Republic

5 May

Nodding your head expresses "yes" in the vast majority of cultures. Be careful though, in Bulgaria, it means what?

"No"

6 May

More vegetarians live in one country than in the rest of the world. Name the country.

India (31% of the population)

7 May

Neckties were first used by which nation?

Croatia, hence their name "cravats" (from the word for Croatian: "hrvat")

8 May

No women or larger-than-cat female animals are allowed in which part of the European Union?

Mount Athos, an autonomous monastic republic within Greece

9 May

In 1712, there was a 30th of February in which country?

Sweden

10 May

Once, an EU country could not form a government for almost two years. Which country?

Belgium

11 May

In some districts of which European country is flushing the toilet after 10 pm against the law?

Switzerland

12 May

The deepest metro station in the world, 105.5m (346 ft.), is in which country?

Ukraine: Kiev's Arsenalna station

13 May

Which African country has far more pyramids than Egypt?

Sudan

14 May

Beer was not considered an alcoholic drink until 2011 in which country?

Russia

15 May

The old walled city of Jerusalem has four quarters: Jewish, Christian, Moslem and...?

Armenian

16 May

When and where did the word Guerrilla originate?

In Spain, during the Napoleonic Wars

17 May

In February 2020, George Hood broke the world planking record with a time of eight hours, 15 minutes, and 15 seconds. He had done around 2,100 hours of planking in preparation. How old was he at the time?

62 years

18 May

A 3-euro coin was emitted by which country?

Slovenia

19 May

One South American historic site attracts over a million tourists each year, although it is hard to reach. Its name is translated as "old mountain". What is its popular name?

Machu Picchu

20 May

When was the first silicone breast implant surgery performed?

1962

21 May

Amphitheatrum Flavium in Rome, Italy, was the original name of which popular amphitheatre?

The Colosseum

22 May

What do cannibals and the Caribbean have in common?

Etymology. Cannibal comes from Christopher Columbus's version of the word Caribs, the name people from the Caribbean called themselves

23 May

When sugar is added to water and dissolved, the volume of the solution stays almost the same, increasing only a little bit. But why? Where has the sugar gone?

As a soluble material is added to a solvent, its molecules become surrounded by the solvent molecules and the volume increases slightly

24 May

What is the largest number that can be expressed with the standard Roman numerals?

3999 (MMMCMXCIX)

25 May

California, Delaware, Florida, Oregon, Idaho, Kansas, Nevada, and New Hampshire are all in Ohio, USA. How is that possible?

They are all towns in Ohio, USA

26 May

US astronauts can vote from space since which year?

1997

27 May

Which is the EU language that has two words for "red"?

Hungarian "piros" and "vörös" both have virtually the same meaning. A bit confusingly, these words are interchangeable in some cases and not in others. Wine is always vörös, for example, while blood or a rose can be either

28 May

Japan's police officers and shop owners use anti-crime colour balls called "bohan yo kara boru". Explain how you imagine they use those balls.

They are paintballs—plastic spheres filled with a brightly coloured liquid pigment—that explode on impact and splash the liquid in a radius of up to 3m (10 ft.). The idea is to throw one after the robber and mark them to improve the chance of an arrest

29 May

How many active volcanoes are there on mainland Europe (excluding islands)?

1, Vesuvius

30 May

In early 2020, amidst the COVID-19 pandemic, Thailand's controversial King Maha Vajiralongkorn self-isolated in a luxury hotel with his "harem" of how many women?

20

31 May

In which European country was it legal to kill Basques (inhabitants of the Basque region of Spain) in the period 1615-2015?

Iceland. It all started in 1615 when a storm destroyed three Basque whaling vessels on an expedition in Iceland. Some eighty members of the crew survived and were left stranded on the island. Having nothing to eat, they resorted to robbing people and raiding farms. The brewing confrontation between locals and the whalers prompted then-sheriff Ari Magnússon to issue a decree that allowed Basques to be murdered with impunity. In the months that followed, about 35 Basques were killed in raids led by the sheriff and local villagers

JUNE

1 June

Which country is named after Jesus?

El Salvador (literally, The Saviour)

2 June

Burrnesha are women who take a vow of chastity and wear male clothing in order to live as men. The sworn virgin is believed to be the only formal, socially defined trans masculine role in Europe. In which countries?

Albania, Kosovo, and Montenegro

3 June

Which is the oldest soda in the world?

Schweppes

4 June

In 1917, US President Woodrow Wilson bought several Caribbean islands for $25 million, renaming them the US Virgin Islands. From which country?

Denmark

5 June

According to the Chinese zodiac, children born in the year of the dragon are more successful in school. Due to the superstition that those born in that year will grow up more successful, places like China, Singapore, and Taiwan typically see a "baby boom" in those years. When was the latest year of the dragon?

2012

6 June

In the USA, there was a so-called Year of Goldfish Gulping. It started out with one live goldfish, swallowed up by a Harvard freshman on a dare. Students at colleges across the country then popularized a quest to see how many goldfish a single person could eat in one sitting. Eventually, the record reached 101 goldfish swallowed. In which year?

1939

7 June

Schweppes is a Swiss beverage brand that is sold around the world. What was it named after?

Its founder, Johann Jacob Schweppe

8 June

A sculpture representing the head of Darth Vader is located on the north, or "dark" side, of a cathedral. In which country?

The United States, at the Washington National Cathedral, Northwest, Washington, D.C.

9 June

In which European country can you see the world's oldest vine, with a confirmed age of over 400 years? It won a place in the Guinness Book of Records as the oldest noble vine in the world still bearing grapes.

Maribor, Slovenia

10 June

Catholic priests in one EU country burned books they consider to be sacrilegious, including those from the Harry Potter series. This happened in the "distant" 2019. Where?

Poland

11 June

The Salem witch trials were a series of prosecutions of people accused of witchcraft in colonial Massachusetts between February 1692 and May 1693. More than two hundred people were accused and many were executed. How many of them were burned at stake?

None. Thirty were found guilty, nineteen of whom were executed by hanging (fourteen women and five men). One other man, Giles Corey, was "pressed to death for refusing to plead", and at least five individuals died in jail

12 June

In English, one letter is contained in the name of all odd numbers. Which one?

The letter "E"

13 June

The Bulgarian Bag, also known as the Bulgarian Training Bag, is a crescent-shaped exercise equipment used in strength training, cardiovascular training, and general physical fitness. It was invented by Bulgarian wrestler, Ivan Ivanov, around 2005 and was inspired by an animal. Which animal?

Sheep and goats. Ivanov was inspired by the tradition of shepherds performing strength acts with sheep and goats on street fairs in his homeland, Bulgaria. The shepherds were often forced to carry lambs and weak sheep on their shoulders when they were wandering with their herds, and were showing off their strength at festivals

14 June

The Tower of London, officially Her Majesty's Royal Palace and Fortress of the Tower of London, is a historic castle located on the north bank of the River Thames in the British capital. A group of at least six captive birds live there and their presence is traditionally believed to protect the Crown and the Tower; a superstition holds that "if they are lost or fly away, the Crown will fall and Britain with it." There is even a full-time position of a caretaker who makes sure the birds feel fine. What species of birds are those?

Ravens

15 June

The roof structures of the Opera House in Sydney are called 'shells'. Their design was one of the most difficult aspects of the building's project. Architect, Jorn Utzon, claimed that the final design of the shells was inspired by peeling a fruit. Which fruit?

Orange

16 June

In early May 2020, who was the celebrity that announced the birth of his son, named X Æ A-12?

Elon Musk

17 June

A driver from Luxembourg received a fine for exceeding the speed limits within the Belgian capital, Brussels. According to the legal document, in early 2018, he had driven with 914 km/h (568 mph) while, "after correction, only xxx has been taken into account for the penalty". What was the final speed that Belgian police wrote on the speed ticket?

859 km/h (534 mph). Apparently, this was due to a technical glitch

18 June

Nowadays, the queen is the most powerful piece in the game of chess. It has not always been called "queen" however. Initially, it was named...? Hint: in some European and Asian languages, it is still called this.

Counsellor or prime minister or vizier

19 June

Ever heard of Siddhattha Gotama (aka Siddhārtha Gautama)? He was a philosopher, meditator, spiritual teacher, and religious leader who lived in ancient India (5 th to 4 th century BCE). Worldwide, he is much better known under another name. What is that name?

The Buddha

20 June

The Sovereign Military Order of Malta, officially the Sovereign Military Hospitaller Order of Saint John of Jerusalem, of Rhodes, and of Malta, commonly known as the Order of Malta or Knights of Malta, is a Catholic lay religious order, traditionally of military, chivalric, and noble nature. The order has been called "the smallest sovereign state in the world". How many citizens does it have?

2

21 June

Erramatti Mangamma from Hyderabad, India, currently holds the record for being the oldest living mother to give birth after conceiving through the process of in-vitro fertilisation. She delivered twin baby girls, which also made her the oldest mother to give birth to twins. How old was she at the time of giving birth?

74

22 June

In 2014, many Americans thought HTML was a type of sexually transmitted disease. What percentage of the US people gave such an answer?

11%. In case you do not know, Hypertext Markup Language (HTML) is the standard markup language for documents designed to be displayed in a web browser

23 June

In 1972, Frenchman Jean Boulet set two records with an Aérospatiale SA 315B Lama helicopter: absolute altitude reached and, as the engine malfunctioned, longest successful autorotation in history (landing a helicopter without working engine). What was the maximum altitude he reached?

12,440m (40,814 ft.)

24 June

Have you ever felt embarrassed? I am sure you have never come close to this: on 8 January 1992, while attending a banquet hosted by the Prime Minister of Japan, Kiichi Miyazawa, the then US President fainted after vomiting in Miyazawa's lap. Who was the US President in question?

US President George H. W. Bush

25 June

Which is the most abundant mineral of Earth's lower mantle [i.e. between 700 and 2900 km of depth (435-1,800 mi.)] that accounts for approximately half of Earth's mass?

(Mg, Fe, Al)(Si, Al)O3, aka perovskite

26 June

African giant pouched rats—huge, cat-sized rodents native to central Africa—have bad vision but an extraordinary sense of smell. They are very efficient in discovering hidden landmines by sniffing out the explosive TNT. One rat can search over 2000 square feet (200 square meters) in 20 minutes, an area that could take a human up to four days. And as if these capabilities were not enough, the rats have also been trained to successfully detect an infectious disease that affects the lungs. Name the disease.

Tuberculosis

27 June

The Kármán line is an attempt to define a boundary between Earth's atmosphere and outer space. How high is it above Earth's surface?

This is important for legal and regulatory measures; aircraft and spacecraft fall under different jurisdictions and are subject to different treaties. There is no international law defining the edge of space, and therefore, the limit of national airspace. The Fédération Aéronautique Internationale (FAI; English: World Air Sports Federation), an international standard-setting and record-keeping body for aeronautics and astronautics, defines the so-called Kármán line as the altitude of 100 kilometres (62 miles; 330,000 ft.) above Earth's mean sea level. Many organizations do not use this definition. For instance, the US Air Force and NASA set the limit to be 50 miles (80 km) above sea level

28 June

Toronto, Canada, used to be called...

York

29 June

How many toes do elephants have on each foot?

6. Not every toe has a corresponding nail though

30 June

Name the world's largest black pepper exporter, accounting for over 60% of global trade.

Vietnam

JULY

1 July

Champagne is a French sparkling wine. As a part of the production process, the secondary fermentation in the bottle causes carbonation and some sediment. How do they remove the sediment without losing the carbonation?

To remove the residue without losing the carbonation, the bottle neck of each bottle is shock-frozen while the bottle is upside down, the residue is thus captured in the block of ice and extracted. Then some wine is added and the bottle closed again. By the way, many people use the term Champagne as a generic term for sparkling wine, but in Europe and some other countries, it is illegal to label any product Champagne unless it comes from the Champagne wine region of France and is produced under the rules of the appellation

2 July

Worldwide, there are over 30,000 golf courses. Which country has the largest number?

As of 2015, there were 15,372 golf courses in the USA. This is 45% of all golf courses in the entire world

3 July

What does ZIP mean?

ZIP is an acronym for Zone Improvement Plan. However, the USPS intentionally chose the acronym to indicate that mail travels more quickly when senders mark the postal code on their packages and envelopes. It makes sense that the term ZIP code would be related to being zippy, which means "lively" or "peppy"

4 July

Worldwide, which country has the highest number of people without religion (atheists and agnostics)?

China, with over 200 million

5 July

Motorola's DynaTAC 8000X was the first commercial portable cellular phone. When was it first marketed?

1983

6 July

One country has a film industry that produces about 50 movies per week, more than Hollywood in the United States and second only to India's Bollywood. Name the country.

Nigeria: The Nigerian film industry is also known as Nollywood

7 July

Madame Tussauds wax museum in London opened in which year?

1835

8 July

In which country do housewives hold 11% of the world's gold, more than the reserves of the IMF, USA, Germany, and Switzerland put together?

India

9 July

How many countries does Spain border?

5. UK, Portugal, France, Andorra and Morocco

10 July

In early June 2020, the Greek Orthodox Church declared one popular sport/spiritual practice 'incompatible' with Christianity. Name it.

The Greek Orthodox Church ruled yoga 'incompatible' with Christianity. Downward dog, sun salutations, and all other yoga practices are "absolutely incompatible" with the Christian faith, the powerful Greek Orthodox Church has said. Yoga has no place "in the life of Christians," the governing body of the Church has ruled

11 July

BASE jumping is the recreational sport of jumping from fixed objects, using a parachute to descend safely to the ground. "BASE" is an acronym that stands for four categories of fixed objects from which one can jump. Name them.

Building, antenna, span, and eart

12 July

What is the only US state with a royal palace?

Hawaii. 'Iolani Palace in downtown Honolulu on the Island of Oahu is the only royal palace in the United States and is a surviving symbol of Hawaiian independence. It was the official residence and capital of the last ruling monarchs of the Kingdom of Hawai'i – King Kalakaua and his sister, Queen Lili'uokalani

13 July

Antoine-Joseph "Adolphe" Sax created the saxophone in the early 1840s, patenting it in 1846. Where was he born?

Dinant, Belgium

14 July

Who was the first Catholic-elected US President?

John F. Kennedy

15 July

In Pakistan, according to the minister of aviation, what is the percentage of pilots who had fake flying licenses as of 2021?

40%

16 July

Pop-up ads were invented by Ethan Zuckerman in which year?

1994. By the way, he later apologised

17 July

How much horsepower is the peak power production of one horse?

It is a common misconception that one horsepower is equal to the peak power production of a horse, which is capable of a maximum of around 14.9 horsepower. By comparison, a human being is capable of approximately five horsepower at peak power production

18 July

In 1958, Bank of America launched BankAmericard, the first card with a "revolving credit" feature. It is now known as which brand of credit cards?

VISA

19 July

In the opening scene of a movie, Mel Gibson demolished for real the old city hall of Orlando, Florida (USA). Name the movie.

Lethal Weapon 3

20 July

A turbojet train is a train powered by jet airplane
engines. Several were built for experimental purposes
in the USA and the USSR, the fastest reaching 296 km/h.
In which year was this speed record set?

1966

21 July

Professor Stephen Hawking threw a Champagne party
complete with Krug and hors d'oeuvres in 2009, and did
not release the invitations until after the party had
taken place. Expectedly, no one attended the party.
What was he trying to prove?

That time travel is not possible

22 July

In 2016, the Malaysian government banned clothing of a certain colour after thousands of protesters wearing such T-shirts demanded the resignation of the Prime Minister. Since then, anyone wearing clothes in this colour can be arrested under the assumption that they are protesting the government. Which colour?

Yellow

23 July

The world's first drive-in movie theatre opened in New Jersey, USA. In which year?

1933

24 July

Substitute x with the missing number (you need to understand the pattern first): 7, 26, 19, 5, 21, 16, 9, x, 4?

13. (26=7+19; 21=5+16; x=9+4)

25 July

The youngest person to travel to all sovereign countries is Alexis Alford. How old was she when she visited the final one?

21

26 July

The Swiss flag is the only square flag flying outside United Nations headquarters in New York as the other country with such a flag is not a member of the international organisation. Which country is that?

Vatican City

27 July

What will happen if you keep an object made of tin at temperatures below -30°C?

It will disintegrate: tin pest is an autocatalytic, allotropic transformation of the element tin, which causes deterioration of tin objects at low temperatures

28 July

Why are flights from west to east faster than the same route traversed in the opposite direction?

Jet streams are, at their most basic, high-altitude air currents caused by atmospheric heating and the inertia of Earth's rotation. They are predominantly west to east

29 July

Which is the best-selling video game franchise (by number of copies sold)?

The Mario series (Super Mario, Mario Kart, Mario Party, Mario Sports), with over 770 million copies sold as of early 2022

30 July

Which is the highest-grossing movie, adjusted for inflation?

Gone with the Wind (1939). As an absolute number, Avengers – Endgame and Avatar had grossed about USD 2.8 billion each as of early 2022

31 July

Most sloths would leave their tree only once a week to do what?

Defecate

AUGUST

1 August

How many countries presently have a head of state holding the title "Emperor"?

1, Japan

2 August

The top three exporters of soy sauce are (1) China, (2) one European country, and (3) Japan. Name the European country that exports more soy sauce than Japan.

The Netherlands

3 August

Which state in the USA has the longest coastline?

Alaska

4 August

How can you visually distinguish between orcas (killer whales) born and living in captivity, and their wild brothers and sisters?

The dorsal fin is only upright when they live free

5 August

Which European country increased its population 12-fold between 1950 and 2010?

Andorra

6 August

Miners used canary birds for what?

Gas detector—canaries die quickly in the presence of methane

7 August

In 2019, Switzerland announced that, for the first time ever, it would mint coins with the face of a living person. Who was the honoured person?

The famous Swiss tennis player, Roger Federer

8 August

In 1993, a US popular singer changed his stage name to an unpronounceable symbol, also known as the "Love Symbol". Who was this singer?

Prince

9 August

When did the USA buy Alaska from the Russian Empire?

1867

10 August

In 2019, an Italian "artist" sold this art installation for the price of USD 120,000. A few days later, the banana was replaced with another one. What happened to the original one?

It was eaten

11 August

Which was the first music video to hit 1 billion views on YouTube in 2012?

Gangnam Style by Psy. By the way, Gangnam is a neighbourhood in Seoul, South Korea

12 August

What is the maximum possible number of Friday the 13ths in a single calendar year?

3

13 August

How many hours is the world's longest regular commercial flight (Los Angeles to Singapore)?

18 hours and 50 minutes

14 August

Which country had the youngest leader worldwide, and as of early 2022, was the only country with a leader below 30 years?

San Marino. Giacomo Simoncini (born 30 November 1994) is one of the country's Captains Regent, along with Francesco Mussoni

15 August

Concrete was known to the ancient world as early as 700 BCE. Ancient Romans used concrete extensively from 300 BCE to 476 CE. After the fall of the Roman Empire, however, mankind quickly "forgot" this technology. When did British engineer, John Smeaton, "reinvent" concrete?

In the 1750s

16 August

In 2019, Russia was banned from all major sporting events by the World Anti-Doping Agency. For how many years?

4

17 August

In 1997, the song "Ironic" was nominated for the Grammy Awards. Ironically, the song's lyrics describe mostly bad luck and not irony. Who performed the song?

Alanis Morissette

18 August

What do the gems Sapphire and Ruby have in common?

They have the same chemical composition

19 August

Tupac Shakur, aka 2Pac, was named after Túpac Amaru II, the 18th-century revolutionary from which Latin American country?

Peru

20 August

Where was the metal copper first mined?

Cyprus. The name "copper" is derived from the Latin "cuprum", which means "metal from Cyprus"

21 August

Alcatraz Island (often referred to as Alcatraz or The Rock) was a maximum-security federal prison 2 km (1.1 miles) off the coast of San Francisco, USA, which operated from 1934 to 1963. Unlike other prisons, inmates were always offered hot showers. Why would the authorities do that?

So that the inmates would get used to hot water and find it impossible to swim through the cold ocean if they wanted to escape

22 August

On 11 September 1875, two teams competed in Springfield, Illinois, USA. Dubbed the Blondes and Brunettes, the players became the first known women to be paid for playing which popular sport?

Baseball

23 August

The melody of the national anthem of the United Kingdom "God Save the Queen" is also used for the national anthem of which European country?

Liechtenstein

24 August

Before plunging into recession due to COVID-19 in 2020, Australia had not experienced one for quite some time. When was the previous economic recession?

1990-1991

25 August

Madison was barely used as a girl's name before 1985. In 2001, it became the second-most-popular name given to female babies in the USA. This surge is generally attributed to the 1984 release of which film?

Splash, starring Tom Hanks and Daryl Hannah

26 August

Coca-Cola was invented by Dr. John S. Pemberton. Towards the end of his life, he reluctantly sold his business as he desperately needed money for what?

He was a drug addict

27 August

What is the capital of Switzerland?

The de facto capital is Bern; however, it is not mentioned in the constitution as such, but barely as "federal city"

28 August

Which is the only airport in the world where scheduled flights use a beach as a runway?

Barra Airport, Scotland

29 August

It used to be a practice to throw a piece of silk against a brick wall. What did it mean if it stuck to the wall and did not slide down?

That it was genuine silk

30 August

The world's longest standing alliance was ratified in 1386 and is still in force. It is between which two countries?

The United Kingdom and Portugal

31 August

How many buffalos (approximately) did Buffalo Bill kill in his life?

0, he killed many bison

SEPTEMBER

1 September

Who was the only Roman Emperor to step down voluntarily?

Lucius Cornelius Sulla Felix (138–78 BCE), commonly known as Sulla

2 September

The Canary Islands were named after an animal. Which one?

Dog

3 September

Until 1951, Catholics were barred from becoming teachers, doctors, or nurses in which EU country?

Sweden

4 September

In 2015, in which country were more citizens killed by toddlers with a gun than by terrorists?

The United States of America

5 September

In some countries, the law recognizes that it is basic human nature to escape and hence the act of escaping itself is not a crime, although you may be punished for any other crime that you commit during your escape. Which countries?

Mexico, Germany, and Austria

6 September

Females of more than 130 species of mammals, as well as of some marsupials can delay the implantation of embryos in their uterus for months, thus timing their babies' birth to a more favourable season. They can put embryos "on hold" for how long?

Up to 11 months

7 September

Who used multiple-choice questions for the first time and why?

US Army, in 1917, to evaluate the military recruits during World War I

8 September

In 1913, which was the dance that virtually everybody worldwide wanted to learn?

Tango

9 September

In 1941, Coca-Cola's brand Fanta was first marketed where?

Nazi Germany

10 September

Today, how many countries have not yet adopted the metric system?

USA, Liberia, and Myanmar

11 September

In Russia, Ukraine, and Bulgaria, men would never give an even number of flowers to a lady. Even number bouquets are reserved for what?

Funerals

12 September

What is the closest distance between Russia and the USA?

4 km (2.5 miles), between the islands Little Diomede (USA) and Big Diomede (Russia)

13 September

Tetris was invented in the Soviet Union. When?

In 1985

14 September

Which country has the southernmost capital in the world?

New Zealand

15 September

The Soviet Union sold PepsiCo 17 submarines, a cruiser, a frigate, and a destroyer in exchange for Pepsi products. For a short period of time, the corporation had the sixth-largest navy in the world. When did it happen?

In 1989

16 September

In 1908, the Russian Olympic team arrived in London, UK, 12 days late. Why?

Russia was still using the Julian calendar. The Russian Orthodox Church still uses it and, therefore, Christmas celebrations in Russia fall on 7 January

17 September

Classic Kinder Surprise chocolate eggs are forbidden in the USA. Why?

It is forbidden to sell food containing non-edible parts hidden inside

18 September

Which is the fastest rotating planet in the Solar system?

Jupiter

19 September

The first hybrid car was built one century earlier than what you most probably think. When?

In 1898, it was patented under the name 'System Lohner-Porsche'

20 September

In the wild, lions are normally found in many African countries. There is, however, a small lion population in one Asian country too. Which country?

India

21 September

Which place in the world changed directionality of traffic twice?

Okinawa, Japan

22 September

The word "Jedi" is derived from which language?

From the Japanese "jidai-geki", meaning Edo period drama

23 September

In 2004, which was the first country in the world to ban the sale and advertisement of baby walkers?

Canada

24 September

Moka/mocca coffee and desserts were named after the city of Mocha. In which country is it located?

Yemen

25 September

Which animal species has its faeces in the shape of a cube?

Wombat

26 September

In 2017, which was the first country to give its citizenship to a robot?

Saudi Arabia

27 September

Soyuz 21 was a 1976 Soviet manned mission to the Salyut 5 space station. It was intended to last more than two months but ended after 49 days in orbit as the two cosmonauts complained about... what?

An insupportable bad odour in the space station

28 September

Some airlines forbid their pilots to grow beards. Why?

***The reason is that an oxygen mask should fit tightly
on the face if an emergency situation occurs. A beard
could prevent this***

29 September

In the 1950s, which US car manufacturer designed a
nuclear-powered tank?

Chrysler

30 September

Which country has the largest parliament with almost
3,000 members?

China

OCTOBER

1 October

In which country was dancing in public outlawed in 1948?

Japan. Technically, today it is only allowed in clubs that have a special permit

2 October

Hippos are not native to Colombia, yet now dozens of feral hippos are bothering Colombian peasants. Where did they come from?

The notorious drug lord, Pablo Escobar, kept them in a private zoo. When he died, they escaped in the wild

3 October

In which country can you marry a dead person?

France. The possibility to marry a deceased person is provided for by Article 171 of the French Civil Code

4 October

Calves of which species grow 2.5 cm (1 inch) a day?

Giraffe

5 October

So far, every bearded US President has been a ... what?

Republican

6 October

When was the decimal point invented?

In the late 16th century

7 October

A necktie can be tied in how many different ways?

85

8 October

Which country is the world's largest producer of false teeth?

Liechtenstein

9 October

Name a country where crucifixion is still one of the official methods of execution?

Sudan, Iran, UAE, Saudi Arabia

10 October

7.5 million Tajiks live in Tajikistan. 10 million Tajiks (i.e. more than those in Tajikistan) live in a neighbouring country. Name the country in question.

Afghanistan

11 October

Japan stopped rice futures trading in 2022. When did it start?

1730

12 October

In 1959, the United States Postal Service experimented with delivering mail using what weapon?

Cruise missile

13 October

Which effect refers to a situation in which a large mass of people believes that an event occurred when it did not?

The Mandela Effect

14 October

Up until 2021, it was possible to rate the Atlantic Ocean on Google Maps. What was the average rating?

3.9*

15 October

In 2021, a robot called Xavier was patrolling the streets and enforcing the anti-COVID measures in which country?

Singapore

16 October

Which country has its geographical centre outside its territory?

Croatia. Check a map

17 October

Which music band was sued by a convicted cannibal?

Rammstein

18 October

Africa and Europe cannot be connected with a bridge or tunnel due to the Gibraltar Strait's depth and the limitations of modern technology. That's a pity as the distance between the two continents is just...

13 km (8.1 mi)

19 October

When was a military helicopter first used in action?

1944

20 October

What has more pizza in it: 1 pizza with a 30 cm diameter or 2 pizzas with a 20 cm diameter each?

1 pizza with a 30 cm diameter

21 October

Ivan Unger and Gladys Roy played tennis on top of a biplane. When did it happen?

1925

22 October

In Sweden, authorities deployed an emergency service called "condom ambulance". In case of need, you could call them for an emergency condom delivery. When did the service start?

2004

23 October

Australian Nathan Grindal was banned from darts tournaments in 2012 and 2013 for one ludicrous reason. He was accused of looking like who?

Jesus Christ

24 October

When did Mike Yurosek invent baby carrots?

1986

25 October

Hindu pilgrims come to the Tirupati Venkateswara Temple to offer a special gift to the god Vishnu. What exactly?

Their hair

26 October

Why did the song "I Am the Walrus" by John Lennon (Beatles) have seemingly incomprehensible lyrics?

John Lennon deliberately wrote nonsense to troll school teachers who analysed Beatles' songs in class

27 October

Historically, long bow shooters had one arm enlarged (longer than the other) and it is still visible on skeletons. Which one?

The right arm

28 October

Which is the most expensive spice in the world by weight?

Saffron spice comes from the crocus flower and has to be handpicked. You would need up to 400,000 flowers to make one kilogram (2 pounds) of saffron. That is why one gram of it can cost as much as EUR 8 (USD 9)

29 October

What was Adolf Hitler's middle name?

He had no middle name

30 October

How many spikes does the crown of the Statue of Liberty have?

7, symbolizing the 7 continents

31 October

Which dessert was named after a Russian ballerina?

Pavlova

NOVEMBER

1 November

What spirit do you use to make a caipirinha?

Cachaça

2 November

What were all these foods named after: Carpaccio, Salisbury steak, Graham cracker, Béchamel sauce, Caesar salad, Peach Melba?

People

3 November

What does the abbreviation IPA stand for in the Food & Drink sector?

India Pale Ale

4 November

Forrest Gump, Jurassic Park, Pulp Fiction, and The Shawshank Redemption were all in the movie theatres at the same time. In which year?

1994

5 November

What is the national dish of Scotland?

Haggis

6 November

What is the shortest film title to win an Oscar for best picture?

The 1958 movie musical, Gigi, and 2012 film, Argo.

7 November

What is the most stolen food in the world?

Cheese

8 November

In which movie sequel does each confidential message auto-destroy after five seconds?

Mission: Impossible

9 November

Which leader from Latin America appeared in two Hollywood movies in his youth?

Fidel Castro

10 November

Fictitious telephone numbers with what prefix are widely used in movies?

555

11 November

In one country, 11 November 2019 was the driest day since weather records began, 137 years ago. Every region of the country had virtually zero rainfall. Name the country.

Australia

12 November

Tulips did not originate in Holland. Where do they come from?

The Ottoman Empire (present-day Turkey)

13 November

Who was the highest paid Hollywood actor in 2021?

Daniel Craig

14 November

Roughly how many varieties of avocado are there?

500

15 November

The World Health Organisation, WHO, skipped two Greek letters while naming COVID variants to avoid political complications. Which ones?

Nu (to avoid jokes with "new") and xi (not to upset the leader of China, Xi Jinping)

16 November

In 2021, Sweden's first-ever female prime minister, Magdalena Andersson, served only...

One day

17 November

On which continent did broccoli originate?

Europe

18 November

Wadi-al-Salaam, lit. 'Valley of Peace', is the largest cemetery in the world, which contains more than 5 million bodies. Where is it located?

Iraq

19 November

Is it left-handed or right-handed people that are more likely to be schizophrenic?

Left-handed

20 November

According to Southeast Asia's folklore and fairy-tales, what animal is there on the Moon?

A rabbit

21 November

Sybil "Queenie" Newall won the gold medal in archery at the 1908 Olympics in London. She is the oldest woman ever to win an Olympic gold medal in an individual event. How old was she?

53 years

22 November

In the 1992 US Presidential elections, what did all three major candidates have in common?

They were left-handed

23 November

In which Asian country do doctors prefer the use of German to that of Latin?

Japan

24 November

Presently, which state in the USA does NOT have a law requiring adult drivers and front-seat occupants to wear seatbelts?

New Hampshire

25 November

Which is the only US state whose motto is in French, "L'Étoile du Nord"?

Minnesota

26 November

What happens to people who die in the northernmost town of the world, Longyearbyen, Norway?

Nobody can be buried if they die there and corpses are transported to the south or cremated

27 November

Which is the largest landlocked country (by population)?

Ethiopia: 112 million as of 2022

28 November

Which is the largest landlocked country (by area)?

**Kazakhstan: 2.7 million square kilometres
(1 million sq. mi)**

29 November

In November 2021, a flight to Zurich was forced to return to Heathrow due to 'the dirty socks smell in the cockpit'. Which airline was it?

Swiss Air

30 November

Both Nelson Mandela and Mahatma Gandhi were independence fighters, both spent time in prison, and both had the same profession. What was it?

Lawyer

DECEMBER

1 December

Derinkuyu is an old underground city. In which modern country is it located?

Turkey

2 December

In China, there are many empty dwellings. Theoretically, these unoccupied flats and houses would be enough for the entire population of which country (as of early 2022)?

France

3 December

When did Ethiopia abolish slavery?

1942

4 December

Which country has the most islands?

Sweden

5 December

While Harry S. Truman was serving as vice president under Franklin Roosevelt, he was not informed about the development of which weapon?

The atomic bomb

6 December

The leading reason for people outside Finland to start learning the Finnish language is...

The enjoyment of Finnish heavy metal

7 December

Which US state has 7.5 million barrels of bourbon and only 4.5 million residents (i.e. more bourbon barrels than people)?

Kentucky

8 December

The horse in Ferrari's logo initially had a tail pointing in which direction?

Down

9 December

All bridges put on euro banknotes were fake (not existing in reality). Then one city decided to build replicas of them all as a tourist attraction. In which country?

The Netherlands

10 December

What was the smallest waist of a person ever recorded?

33 cm (13 inches)

11 December

As of 2022, the SR-71 continues to hold the official world record for the fastest manned aircraft. The record was set in which year?

1976

12 December

Which country has the longest national constitution in the world (146,385 words)?

India

13 December

In 1771, King Gustav III of Sweden thought one beverage was dangerous and ordered a human study on two identical twins. He commuted the death penalty for the crime committed by them to life imprisonment if they participated in his experiment: one had to drink the "dangerous" substance each day, the other not. What substance are we talking about?

Coffee

14 December

What live animal did Russians put in milk to keep it fresh?

A brown frog. Historically, Russians believed that putting a frog in their milk would keep it fresh. A recent study proved that some chemicals in the frog's skin indeed inhibit the growth of bacteria and fungi

15 December

As of early 2022, what was the most-viewed YouTube video, with over 10 billion views?

"Baby Shark Dance"

16 December

His famous horse logo was given to Enzo Ferrari as a gift. Before it became a symbol of sports cars, it was used by who?

An Italian WWI military pilot

17 December

Persia was renamed to Iran in which year?

1935

18 December

Forty camels were disqualified from a beauty pageant in Saudi Arabia in late 2021. Why?

Officials realized the camels had received Botox and fillers to appear more beautiful

19 December

Only two national flags use the colour purple. They are both in America. Name any of the countries.

Dominica and Nicaragua

20 December

The longest constitution in the world is that of one US state (388,882 words long). Which one?

The state of Alabama, USA

21 December

Airplane inventors, the Wright brothers, did not have a college degree (although their sister and parents did). For one full year, no journalist showed interest and the first US article describing their invention appeared in a journal for... beekeepers! Years later, they became celebrities in another country and first sold airplanes to this country's army. Name the country.

France

22 December

The Greek king, Alexander, died in 1920, following a bite from what animal?

Monkey

23 December

What did Hitchcock use for blood in the shower scene of Psycho?

Chocolate syrup

24 December

Burj Khalifa, Dubai (UAE) is the tallest building in the world. What size is the tube connecting it to the central canalization?

It is notorious for not being connected to a canalisation

25 December

Baileys Irish Cream is an Irish cream liqueur—an alcoholic drink flavoured with cream, cocoa, and Irish whiskey. In which year was it first marketed?

1974, thus much later than what most people think...

26 December

According to the Islamic tradition, (1) one should enter a mosque with which foot, and (2) exit the mosque with which foot?

According to the Islamic tradition, (1) one should enter a mosque with their right foot, and (2) exit the mosque with their left foot

27 December

Starting from the 16th century up until the present day, some superstitious doctors would write "Σ" instead of which disease?

Syphilis

28 December

Stephanie Matto, a former reality TV actress from the USA, makes $45,000 (USD) weekly by selling jars that contain samples of what?

Her farts

29 December

Who was the only US President to serve two non-sequential terms so far?

Grover Cleveland

30 December

Camels walk moving which legs together?

***The first two legs from one side (for instance left),
then two from the other side (right)***

31 December

Which famous singer was offered the leading role in the
"Die Hard" film series? He turned it down and Bruce
Willis accepted...

Frank Sinatra

VERIFICATION PROCESS

To start with, however a great read Wikipedia is, I have never used it to confirm facts; I instead checked the sources listed there and evaluated them.

Anything science-related like "Which is the fastest rotating planet in the Solar system?" would need to be confirmed by at least two (preferably three) separate scientific publications, be it on paper or online of the sort of

http://www.science.gov/,

http://www.nasa.gov/,

http://www.britannica.com/,

http://www.sciencemag.org/,

https://www.newscientist.com/,

https://www.genome.gov/education/,

http://www.howstuffworks.com/,

http://www.merriam-webster.com/.

The scientific publications and websites of the best universities worldwide are also consistently checked (excerpt from the list): University of Cambridge, Stanford University, University of Oxford, California Institute of Technology, Massachusetts Institute of Technology,

Harvard University, Princeton University, Imperial College London, ETH Zurich – Swiss Federal Institute of Technology, Yale University, Columbia University, University of Toronto, Humboldt University of Berlin, University of Tokyo, Heidelberg University, University of Melbourne, Peking University etc.

For events or facts of the type "Forty camels were disqualified from a beauty pageant in Saudi Arabia in late 2021. Why?", I checked at least three reputable newspaper articles and confirmed television reports. Example for newspapers/TV channels used to verify events: The New York Times, Washington Post, Wall Street Journal, The Guardian, The Economist, Financial Times, Times of India, Le Monde, The Sydney Morning Herald, Frankfurter Allgemeine Zeitung, Bloomberg, Al Jazeera, Reuters, Associated Press, BBC, TV5 MONDE, CNN, etc.

ACKNOWLEDGEMENTS

This book is dedicated to my family: my loving wife, Anna, my curious and restless sons, Pavel and Nikolay, and my mother, Maria, who sparked my interest in reading. Thank you for being so patient with me during the lengthy process of writing. You are my inspiration!

Many thanks to all test readers, friends, and colleagues who provided vital feedback and constructive criticism.

ZEALOUS TEST READERS

Alexandra Oliveira-Jones

Alexandra Sandu

Andrea Leitenberger

Brian Power

Daniela Pfaltz

Dimitar Dimitrov

Eva Goulas

Istvan Kovacs

Jess Bauldry

Kalina Simeonova

Linda Van Ras

Marina Heda

Robert Pernetta

Tamina Tietz

ABOUT THE AUTHOR

Born in Bulgaria, I have lived in places like Germany, Belgium, and Iraq, before settling down with my family in Luxembourg. With varied interests, I have always suffered from an insatiable appetite for facts stemming from an unrestrainable intellectual curiosity. It has undoubtedly influenced my academic background and career: after acquiring Master degrees in Greek Philology, German and English Translation, I graduated in Crisis Management and Diplomacy, and most recently undertook an MBA. Member of MENSA.

My career has been equally broad and diverse, swinging from that of an army paratrooper and a military intelligence analyst; through to that of a civil servant with the European Commission, and presently, that of a clerk, performing purely financial tasks in a major bank.

My hobbies include scuba diving, travelling, and learning foreign languages.

MY BOOKS ON AMAZON

1123 Hard To Believe Facts

Which Is NOT True? - The Quiz Book

Fascinating Facts for the Whole Family
(also in audio format)

853 Hard To Believe Facts

523 Hard To Believe Facts (also in audio format)

323 Disturbing Facts about Our World

463 Hard To Believe Facts

CONNECT WITH NAYDEN KOSTOV

Email: n.kostov@raiseyourbrain.com
Twitter: @RaiseYourBrain
Instagram: RaiseYourBrain

I hope you have enjoyed this book. I would greatly appreciate it if you would write your honest review on Amazon and GoodReads.

You could also check out my other books and download a free sample from my website www.RaiseYourBrain.com:

1123 Hard To Believe Facts
Which Is NOT True? - The Quiz Book
Fascinating Facts for the Whole Family
853 Hard To Believe Facts
523 Hard To Believe Facts
323 Disturbing Facts about Our World
463 Hard To Believe Facts

There you could also subscribe to my newsletter and learn first about my future projects